RANDOM RHAPSODIES

A COLLECTION OF POEMS CAPTURING THE CASCADE OF LIFE'S MYRIAD MOMENTS

SONAL BHATIA RANDHAWA

Made with ♥ on the Notion Press Platform
www.notionpress.com

St.Patrick's Junior College, Agra, India

To my beloved Alma mater for nurturing my love for words and the arts

The place where my journey into the world of poetry commenced.

Contents

Contents

Contents

Preface

"Random Rhapsodies", is a journey through the labyrinth of human emotions, experiences, and reflections. This collection of poems seeks to capture the essence of life's myriad moments, from the profound solitude of self-discovery to the bittersweet nostalgia of cherished memories. Each poem is a window into the soul, offering glimpses of the struggles, joys, fears, and triumphs that shape our existence.

As you delve into these verses, you will encounter stories of love and loss, hope and despair, clarity and confusion. The poems traverse a wide emotional landscape, reflecting the complexities and contradictions of life itself.

Whether it is the poignant yearning of a mother, the serene embrace of nature, or the haunting echoes of past relationships, these poems invite you to pause, reflect, and find solace in the beauty of expression.

Sonal Bhatia Randhawa

Acknowledgements

"Grateful To the Miraquill Team and their fellow poets community for prompting,encouraging and Inspiring"

1. **Solitude**

She thought she was standing with everyone, but
When she looked around, she found no one beside her.
Solitude gave her a peaceful abode.
The chaotic world could not reside her!

2. **Cryptic**

The alleyway is dark,
The shadows are stark,
The noise is deafening,
The crowd is maddening.
She stands in a lonely corner,
There is no soul beside her.
As the crowd approaches near,
She can feel the crippling fear.
She wants to run far and far,
But her legs have no power.
In vain she stretches out her hand,
But there is no one who can understand.
She waits and waits for someone to hold,
Her story remains forever untold.

3. **A Mother's Yearning**

As I fumble through your pictures,
I keep telling myself, "No, I don't miss you, but…"
I miss scrambling my way through the scattered books on the
floor.
I miss searching for things in the maze of clothes hanging
through the ever-open wardrobe door.
I miss the random posters of weird-looking "stars" on the walls.
I miss the red and white guitar and the green tennis balls.
I miss the cacophony that you called the song of your favorite
rock star.
I miss the constant blabbering from the back seat of my car.
I miss the crumpled bedsheet on your cluttered bed,
Which amazingly always had space for you to sleep.
I miss the constant alarm in the morning going,
Beep beep.
I miss the empty pizza boxes and the cans creating an ugly sight.
Our constant arguments on this landing into a useless fight.
And when I call you now, though I always seem in jest,
But deep inside my heart… yearn to say,
"Fly back home, my little one, come back to my empty nest."

4. **From Mother to Daughter**

When I first saw you like a tiny dot on the screen,
The first sign of life, your invisible heart pulsating,
My heart leaped with joy.
When I felt your first kick in my abdomen,
Your playful movement inside me felt pleasure, not pain.
When you came into this world
And I heard your first cry,
I forgot all the agony I went through. When you gave your first
social smile,
Your tiny lips separating like rose petals,
Flowers bloomed in my heart.
You took your first step,
Fumbling while trying to balance on your tiny feet.
My heart skipped a beat.
As I rushed to hold you in my arms,
My foot twisted, but I could not let you get hurt.
Oblivious of my pain, I reached you.
Now you are a grown-up girl, but still, you are my little darling.
Even now,
When I see you trotting around,

My heart leaps with joy.
Even now,
When I see you enjoying and having fun,
I feel the same pleasure.
Even now,
No matter how severe, my aches and pains vanish.
When I see you in pain.
Even now,
When you fumble on any step in life,
My heart skips a beat.
But trust me, my child,
Even now,
I will not let you fall ever,
Despite any twists or turns I might face. You just need to have
the same faith in me,
As you had as a child.

5. **Afternoon of Life**

Forties and fifties are confusing,
Seems like teenage again.
Not young but not old too.
The names you don't remember, but the memories come so
clear…
Loud music seems deafening, but silence is so frightening.
Aunties don't go to the disc,
Your children advise you. Yogasans and meditations do not at all
entice you.
Bright colors are oh so garish!
And pastels! I look more auntyish. Fast food is no no! Bad for
health! But low carb, low fat are so eeww!
Work is tiring, but then if no work,
Oh oh! I am bored. What should I do!
No me time :(Lots of people around,
Sitting alone. Oh! I feel so left out. At times, the past haunts you,
and at times, the future worries!
But still, It is the age which finally defines you,
Gives the freedom to just be YOU!
Allows you to dig up lost passions that had long been buried
Amidst the materialistic gravel.
The little mystic pleasures of life, You again begin to unravel!

6. **Melancholia**

A dark well,

She sits at the bottom.

The high walls imposing, she stretches out her hand, but darkness

engulfs it.

She calls out for help, but the walls return it.

And she slowly withers…

But no one bothers…

For none ever peeped, no rays of light seeped. She waited and

waited.

7. **Certainty of the Uncertain**

There is a strange certainty about all that is uncertain.
The occult, the obscure.
I close the doors of my mind,
but it still creeps in through the narrow openings…
That sound…
Is it my heartbeat?
Is it the ticking of the clock? Or someone's footsteps?
That moving curtain…
Is it the wind?
Is it my shadow?
Or is there someone behind it?
The phone ringing…
Is it a friend?
Is it a colleague? Or just a wrong number?
The beads of sweat…
Is it fear?
Is it anxiety? Or imminent cardiac arrest?
The certainty of the uncertain,
Scary or enticing?

8. **Who loved Krishna more?**

Who loved Krishna more?

Radha or Rukmini?

The one who got her beloved or the one who gave away her beloved…

The one who gave happiness to Krishna…

Or the one who gave up her happiness for Krishna…

The one who was always in Krishna's heart…

Or the one who always kept Krishna in her heart…

The one who was forever with Krishna…

Or the one who had Krishna forever.

The one who got everything from Krishna…

Or the one who gave up everything for Krishna.

The one whom the world always remembers with Krishna…

Or the one who forgot her own identity for Krishna.

So who loved Krishna more? Radha or Rukmini?

9. **Shivani**

Shiva took poison, but I took his blues.
Rama went to "vanwas" (exile).
I followed through.
Krishna did "raas" (dance-drama).
I sat in silence.
In Mahabharata (a Hindu epic),
I was blamed for violence.
Carrying the load
Of "honour" on my head,
Sacrificing, tolerating, adjusting till I am dead?

10. O Night!

O Night!
Cradle me in your arms.
Let my fears rest on your bosom.
Gently embrace my darker thoughts.
In the darkness, let them be lost.
O Night!
Cradle me in your arms,
Hide my anxieties in the dark crevices Of the faraway moon.
Let the moonlight bathe me in calmness.
O Night!
Cradle me in your arms.
Wash away my ugly memories with the cascading tears.
Heal my scathing wounds with your soothing hands.
O Night!
Cradle me in your arms…
Rock me like a baby.
Let the moon rays caress me to sleep,
And then…
let my eyes open
To a new dawn!

11. **A Slice Of Sky **

I picked up a slice of sky from my past,
Shunted out the dark clouds that dotted it.
The sun of wisdom stood shining bright.
I flew like a nimble-winged bird in search of my own horizons,
The ones that would be mine forever!

12. **Life**

Twisted trails,
Haunting heights,
Blistering blaze,
Flummoxing flights.
Convoluted caves,
Treacherous trenches,
Wuthering waves,
Breaking benches.
Limitless ladder,
Steady strife,
Missing maps,
Lonely life!

13. **Petals in My Journal**

The rose petals in my journal have dried into shades of brown,
And your photographs in my drawer haven't tasted air for years now.
But the whiff of your sweet-smelling hair still haunts me.
Your tinkling laughter echoes like soft melody in my ears.
Your gentle fingers still seem to be entwined with my crooked ones.
When I write, you seem to be whispering the words into my ears.
The rose petals and the photographs may be dull and faded,
But memories…they will always be fresh and vivid…

14. **Last dove**

As the last dove flew away
I saw the cage door sway.
As if bidding adieu in joy,
Liberating to soar in the open sky.
Contented to have set her free,
And see her flying away in glee.
The empty cage though feels pain,
Wishes no bird is ever caged again!

15. **The Autumn Winds**

The autumn winds,
The dry leaves,
Separated, broken.
The nude trees,
Tired and shaken,
Desperately waiting for the arrival of spring!

16. **I am...**

I Am...

A serene river,

Flowing down rocky terrains.

A cool breeze,

Passing through high mountains.

A bounded bird,

Wishing to soar in the open sky.

A curious cat,

Sometimes trying to peek and pry.

A wounded healer,

Trying to balm others' sores with mine.

An exploring wanderer,

Crossing the darkness and seeking sunshine.

A calm warrior,

Combating, losing, or winning my inner strife.

A blinded sleuth,

Solving the cryptic clues of the enigma called life.

17. **The Drowsy Flower**

The drowsy flower wearily gathered her petals,
as she saw the sun waving goodbye.
She felt as if the darkness would devour her,
but then came the Silver Moon, wrapped her in his arms and
whispered softly,
"Do not worry, the night is not here to stay,
I shall be your color of hope till the sun shines again."

18. **Rather**

*I would rather stitch poems with threads of your memories than
sew my tattered heart.*
*I would rather reminisce and relish the moments spent with you
than rue over why we fell apart.*
I would rather look forward than cry over what you left behind.
*I would rather fast forward the film we made together than
rewind.*
I would rather await the morning sun than hide in the darkness.
I would rather search for a road than perish in wilderness.

19. **Not All Poems Are Meant to Be Read**

Not all poems are meant to be read.
Some are just bittersweet concoctions of emotions,
Brewed up in your heart, awaiting to be poured out.
Hidden away from others but
Intoxicating you like old wine.

20. **Phoenix**

They burn me with their hatred,
I rise like a phoenix from the ashes.

21. **Rain Drops Go Pitter Patter**

Rain drops go pitter patter.
The wind swooshes by.
The leaves softly chatter,
As the waves gently splash
Over the whispering shores.
Slowly the sand castles crash.
Monsoon hums a lullaby
When the clouds thunder,
To calm the restless angry sky.

22. **Storm by the Sea**

The raging waves,
Lashing at the hapless shore.
The jittery leaves,
Desperately clinging to the shivering trees.
The furious clouds thundering,
The flashes of light,
Threatening and intimidating.
The sea shells fumbling,
The boats all tumbling.
Scorned by humans,
Nature loses patience,
Rebels with a vengeance.

23. **The Clock**

The clock hands run tick tick.
Don't stop! Move on quick quick!
The clock alarm goes tring tring.
Lost time no one will again bring!
The clock battery goes beep beep.
Act fast, you have promises to keep!
The clock is wound round and round.
What goes away never comes around!
The clock on the wall or on the table,
Keeps us moving though it's stable!

24. **The Night Was Dark**

The night was dark.
There was no spark.
She could not sleep.
No one could hear her weep.
Her fears became stark as
The night was dark.
On old memories she stumbled,
That had made her life jumbled.
She wanted to break away,
But she could not find a way.
The night was dark.
There was no boat to embark.
She desperately looked around,
But no anchor to her soul she found.
Darkness devoured her like a shark.
The night was dark.

25. **'Tell Me**

Tell me when the sun goes down,
Will you be my light?
Tell me when I lose my wings,
Will you be my flight?
Tell me when I lose my way,
Will you be my guide?
Tell me when I feel defeated,
Will you be my pride?
Tell me when I fall down tired,
Will you be my prop?
Tell me when I get impulsive,
Will you say "No! Stop!" Tell me you will always be there,
If ever I feel insecure.
I seek you to be forever beside me,
Nothing less or more!

26. **Little Treasures**

My Enid Blytons and Famous Fives
The Nancy Drews and Hardy Boys,
The ugly rag doll,
The bright red ball,
Some crayon pieces,
Sand castles on beaches,
The rope swings,
The rubber rings,
That paper boat,
In the muddy moat,
My little treasures as a child,
Lost forever in the daily grind,
As the years slowly unwind.
So much gets left behind.

27. **Sail on the Paper**

I can sail on the paper,
Placidly rowing my pen
Over the waves of emotions,
Ebbing and recovering.
Touching the shores
Of all that I dream of,
And anchoring where
My yearnings end.
I

28. **Desires**

I desire solitude,
Yet stay in a crowd.
I desire fluidity,
Yet hold my ground.
I desire dizzying heights,
Yet have steady feet.
I desire anonymity,
Yet want people to greet.
I desire comforts galore,
Yet live like a sage.
I desire to be young forever,
Yet not defy my age.
I desire no contradictions,
Yet I cannot agree.
I desire love to chain me,
Yet I want to be free.
Life indeed is confusing,
Yet we carry through.
Accept and move ahead,
Do not crib or rue!

29. Brewing Poetry

As long as I can brew my words into poetry,
My heart will always be filled to the brim.

30. **Ocean Inside Your Eyes**

There's a serene ocean inside your eyes
Where my dreams float along with yours.
Where the pearls of my desires lie cocooned,
Where my mystical future lies hidden in the sands of time.
While I stand waiting on the shore,
To be swept away and drowned forever.

31. **Autobiography of a Mirror**

I stand glued to the wall in your room,
Hanging in there all by myself,
Yet, I am never alone.
Howsoever one may camouflage,
I can always see through.
I capture it all,
Be it the feel-good days or the bad hair days.
I am that most truthful friend,
Who loves you unconditionally and unapologetically.
However, I am fragile,
So please handle me with care.
Some days you forget to clean me,
That makes everything look hazy to both of us.
A gentle wipe is all it needs.
Remove the dust and stains and behold, I am like new again.
Trust the reflection you see in me,
Take it to be the best!

32. **An Ordeal**

I am on a cleaning spree.
Get set go! One, two, and three.
The wardrobes stand disrobed,
Their every corner keenly probed.
The heap of clothes on the floor jeer,
"Who is now going to put us back, dear?"
The window sills need to be dusted,
Oh! Let me clean the latches rusted.
Oh no! The clothes on the floor are gathering dust.
Let me put them in the cupboard first.
The clothes go back into their piles,
I feel tired as if I walked a hundred miles.
The stubborn stain on the coffee table making a face,
I rub and rub it till it leaves no trace.
Now it's time for me to broom and mop the floor,
Sorry, too exhausted now, I cannot do it anymore.
The house is more of a mess now than before,
As I lie drained out and sprawled on the dusty floor.
In minutes I was snoring away to glory,
And herein ends my cleaning story!

33. **Thank You, My Friend**

When I fumbled,

When I stumbled,

When I jumbled,

When I grumbled,

You were always there!

When I cried,

When I lied,

When I shied,

When I tried,

You were always there!

When I smiled,

When I viled,

When I riled,

When I piled,

You were always there!

When I smoked,

When I choked,

When I joked,

When I soaked,

You were always there! Thank you, my friend!

34. **Perspective**

I built a house,
With bricks and mortar.
Painted it in myriad colours,
Standing tall but lifeless!
I built a home,
With trust and affection.
Wrapped it up with vivid emotions,
Standing firm and alive forever!

35. **Her Strange Madness....**

Her strange madness for scribbling emotions on paper
kept her sane even in the most turbulent times …
and people called it poetry!

36. **Poems Are Silken Threads**

Poems are silken threads of words,
Words that bind a million hearts.
Hearts tattered and torn by pain,
Pain is where the poetry starts.

37. **The Paint on the Walls**

The paint on the walls of the old house was slowly chipping off,
just like the hearts of the old couple who lived there,
Both abandoned by the ones they had once sheltered.

38. **One Foggy Winter Night**

One foggy winter night
As the lone lamp shines bright,
Carving out sharp silhouettes
from the sheets of obscurity,
Hope emerges!

39. **Love Is...**

Love is not magic,
Yet it casts a spell.
An enamouring euphoria,
An enchanting enigma,
A devastating delusion,
Sometimes a social stigma.
Culminated, it's heaven,
When lost, it's hell.

40. **Crowded Chaotic Cauldron**

The city was like a crowded chaotic cauldron of crazy creatures,
jostling, jumping and juggling
in an obnoxiously obstinate overdrive to outdo each other.

41. **A Glass Castle on the River Side**

A glass castle on the riverside,
A majestic black stallion to ride,
Candy floss clouds floating by,
The cuckoos singing a lullaby.
Dew drops covered green meadows,
The dainty flowers dancing in rows,
And you walking beside me hand in hand,
Forever and ever on the moonlit sand.

42. Most Beautiful Poems

Sometimes the most beautiful poems are created
when the wounds in your heart ooze
and your pen gently wipes them off with words.

43. **Nirvana**

As she pranced around,
In the wilderness,
The sublime moonlight
Wrapped up her tired soul,
And balmed it gently.
The drunken breeze
Merrily blew away
The dark veil off her
Forbidden desires.
The dry rustling leaves
Cushioned and soothed
Her exhausted feet.
The cascading river
Played a lilting melody,
Drowning the cacophony
That had long hurt her ears.
And she danced in bliss,
Celebrating her liberation.
Liberation from the shackles
She had built herself.

44. **Ode to Chocolate**

Alluringly dark,
With a soft mushy core.
As it breaks with a crackle,
An intoxicating whiff
Fills up the nostrils.
A bittersweet cascade gently quenches the parched taste buds,
And lands you in transcendental euphoria!

45. **Spring is not Far**

When the leaves turn brown,
It's time to let the withered memories fall.
Let the autumn breeze blow them away into oblivion.
Let your heart be disrobed, raw and naked in anticipation like
the leafless trees
That wait patiently for the birth of the new leaves.
Autumn will soon be over and the spring is not far!

46. **The Blank Pages**

I search for an answer in the blank pages
To all the questions that were never asked,
To all the words that were never spoken,
To all the emotions that remained encased within,
To all the false perceptions that were made,
To all the feelings that you did not communicate,
Wish you had written a few words to express what you felt,
You just left, leaving the blank pages on the table.
No questions asked, no answers given!

47. **Wanderlust**

48. **At times we love the mess**

Cleanliness is next to Godliness
But at times we truly love the mess:
Books spread on the floor,
Clothes hanging on the door,
A guitar lying lazily on the bed,
The wrinkled bedsheet partly spread,
The poster-laden wall with chipped-out paint
Of some game characters that look so quaint,
Some dried leaves on the window sill,
A few specks of dust on the balcony grill.
I miss that mess since the day you left.
Come back, my child, to my empty nest.
The house is clean, but I want a mess.
For me, the mess is next to godliness.

49. **Wrapped in an Envelope**

Wrapped in an envelope,
Kept in my table drawer:
Some stolen memories,
Few broken dreams,
Some hidden desires,
An unsolved maze,
A bunch of regrets,
Unaccomplished tasks,
Unfulfilled commitments,
Unkept promises,
All to be burnt one day,
Mingled with my ashes.

50. **Reunion**

Life is a barren field frozen with snow,
But old friends make the sun glow.
When a desolate man wrapped in silence,
Looking for light in a sea of darkness,
Meets his old friends at a school reunion,
Life again seems to be full of fun.
Their croaky voices heard after years,
The noise is music to his ears.
Laughing, jumping, dancing like clowns,
No cares, no tears, no fears, no frowns.
There is a strange sanity in the madness,
Like a laugh in the sea of sadness!